D0611193

HILAIRE BELLOC

HILAIRE BELLOC

HILAIRE BELLOC

An Introduction
to his
Spirit and Work

by

ROBERT HAMILTON

DOUGLAS ORGAN
140 STRAND, LONDON, W.C.2

First published, 1945
Second edition, 1947

By the same author
W. H. HUDSON: THE VISION OF EARTH

To my wife, Margaret

47561

824
B41zh

FOREWORD

A famous critic once complained that Belloc's work lacks a centre. The work of most writers, he said, is like a planetary system: no matter how diverse in content, it revolves around a centre that imparts unity and strength to the whole. Now I think that if we change the metaphor from the astronomical to the biological field we shall see that the criticism is not altogether justified. Belloc's work is extremely diverse, but like the diversity of nature it is informed by an *élan vital* that imparts to it a living unity. This *élan vital*—the spirit of Belloc—is Catholic humanism, and it is the key to the understanding and full appreciation of the work. But even the work itself is far less diverse than is generally believed. In point of fact it falls into four broad divisions: history, sociology, essays (including miscellaneous works), and verse; and these four are in turn related, not only by the inner spirit of Catholic humanism, but by its external application. In his historical writings, Belloc deals with human nature in the past: in his sociological writings, with human nature in the present; and both are treated intellectually. But in the essays and miscellaneous writings, this corpus of knowledge overflows into a free expression of a profound human sympathy which in the verse finds its most sensitive and aesthetic expression.

Nevertheless the variety and quantity of the work does raise very real problems to the critic. So complex an output demands simplification, and it is necessary to give the reader a broad grasp of the work as a whole. In order to clarify the argument I have provided a synopsis; and as a complement to the argument I have appended a complete list of Belloc's works in the form followed in the argument: history, sociology, essays and miscellaneous works, and verse. I do not doubt that some day a definitive critical biography of Belloc will be produced. Meanwhile I hope this Introduction will serve a useful purpose.

Bedford 1943

CONTENTS

THE HUMANIST

THERE is a story told of Hilaire Belloc—it is probably untrue—that in the exuberant days of his youth he walked into a famous restaurant, and pointing to a harmless looking individual in a corner, said to the assembled company, " Look at that man," and then proceeded to recount the great deeds he had done. Afterwards, on being asked who the man was, Belloc replied that he had not the faintest idea. Now the point of this story, apart from its absurdity, is that all his life and in all his work Belloc has been saying, " Look at that man— and at this man—and at *everyman.*" His work is a mirror of the human spirit.

Humanism, in whatever form, is a concrete thing, and the power and vitality of Belloc's work proceeds from his concrete grasp of human affairs. His concern is with the Faith *in act*, in its relation to human personality and society, with the historical fact of Christ's existence and of the Church He founded. "The essence of Christianity," says Windelband, "is the conception of personality and the relation of person to person as the very kernel of reality." While far from ignoring the mystical and metaphysical, Catholic teaching insists that the Church, and the life and claims of the Founder, are objective facts resting upon ascertainable *evidence*. Taking the Gospels provisionally as ordinary historical documents, the enquirer first asks himself whether they present sufficient evidence for their credibility; and having established that they do, he goes on to enquire into the evidence for Christ's claim to be God, and for the Catholic claim that He founded an infallible Church. It is upon this, not upon mystical experience or metaphysical speculation, that the Faith rests. The mystical and the speculative follow, do not precede, the evidence for the truth and genuineness of the Church. This central Catholic attitude (admirably brought out in such books as Arnold Lunn's *The Third Day* and Knox's *Belief of Catholics*) is a stumbling block to many genuinely religious people tainted with subjectivism. But without it, Christianity would be like a house built upon sand.

Belloc has repeatedly urged the evidence for the Faith; and a small but significant part of his work deals with Catholic apologetics, mostly through the channel of history. For science he has little use—although his debate with Wells showed him to be well read in the subject. Science is too remote for a man of such deeply human sympathies; and I fancy that if he had much interest in the subject it would be in applied science.

Like most humanists, Belloc is a sceptic; for scepticism follows from knowledge of men and their ways. He is the least gullible of men; and his common sense, logic, and realism give strength to his judgments. From his scepticism proceeds his irony, which is saved by the Faith from ever degenerating into contempt. Perhaps the most attractive feature of his personality is a unique synthesis of scepticism, irony, worldliness, and faith. Typically, he expresses a preference for the ontological argument for the existence of God over all others. This so-called ontological argument which is really a psychological argument, argues from the *idea* of a perfect Being to His reality. It finds the starting point for the existence of God in man rather than, as does the cosmological argument, in the world; in human nature rather than in nature.

The humanist mentality is an inborn gift, a sympathy; but humanism is also a way of life, vaguely realized to some extent in all communities, though flourishing only under the influence of some favourable creed or political system. Where the predominant philosophy is unfavourable, humanism is either despised, as in the Orient, or attacked, as in the modern totalitarian States. Oriental transcendentalism regards human personality as essentially evil, and seeks to transcend it in the impersonal One: man has no value as man but only as the possessor of certain ethical qualities that reflect the One in him. This attitude of the Orient is the cause of what the West regards as her inertia; her lack of drive. At the other extreme we get mechanist totalitarianism, the Western philosophy of energy, which regards man as a bundle of conditioned reflexes having meaning and coherence only in the social economic machine. Each tends to lead to the other by re-action; and both end in irrationality. Transcendentalism ends in subjectivism; materialism ends in mechanistic determinism. Thus in neither an inhuman transcendentalist society nor a sub-human mechanist society can the humanist spirit flourish.

There seem to have been only two genuinely humanist societies in the history of the world: the pagan society of ancient Greece and Rome, and the Christian society that followed. It is not, then, surprising to find that Belloc is profoundly moved by the classical spirit. Pagan and Christian humanism have much in common, as we see from the traditions of the public school and university, where the classics and Christian doctrine are (or used to be) regarded as fundamental to the education of a fully integrated personality.

It would, however, be fatal to overlook the wide distinction between pagan and Christian humanism. Paganism was built upon the natural man; Christianity upon the supernatural man. The pagan humanist emphasized the free, natural man who, though the summit of nature, is never more than a part of nature. For the pagan humanist the supernatural, in the full Christian sense, did not exist; but there did exist an extra-natural emanation of gods, themselves half human, who along with the stars and other purely natural forces, ruled the destiny of man. Side by side with this extra-*natural* world of popular belief went the extra-*rational* forms of philosophical thought. But religion, with all its myths, preserved the humanist centre while philosophy moved steadily away from it.

Christianity was founded upon the best in the pagan world; but it affirmed a new and revolutionary humanism centred in Christ. It brought into the world the conception of the supernatural man having his roots in earth, and drawing his breath from God through the living Church incorporated into society. For the pagan humanist, man was God; for the Christian humanist, God was man. The tremendous fact of the Incarnation produced what M. Maritain calls *humanisme intégral;* the humanism of the Catholic Church. The divine humanity of Christ is the direct inspiration of this at once personal and social view of man. It is true that all religions are, to some extent, centred in their founder; but the Christian religion is not only centred in Christ as teacher, but integrated in Him as person. Without minimizing the importance of what He taught and what He did—His death, above all—we must not forget that His ultimate significance for us is what He *is*.

It is impossible to overstress the importance of the Christian teaching on the integrated dual nature of human personality. All other teachings about human nature tend to fall into the error of simplification; to regard man either as part of the One, the Idea, as do the transcendentalists, or as part of an energy system, as do the materialists. Like opposed gravitational fields upon the central force of concrete humanity, these two tendencies are for ever exercising their disintegrative pull; but they can never entirely succeed, for their ineffectiveness is shown whenever we attempt to use them to explain and interpret our common experience.

The modern world has tended to move away from the joyous spirit of Christian humanism; and with this tendency has gone an emasculation of the spirit. The pagan ideal of the complete man, full of joy in life, not given to excess but holding a balanced tension between the intellectual, imaginative, emotional and volitional forces of his nature, was closer to the Christian position than is generally admitted. The Christian—as in the shining example of St. Francis—enjoyed life in Christ.

There has grown up in certain quarters a view of the Christian as either conventional, or as an enthusiast. It is true that Christianity has at different times produced these types; but neither is the mark of the Catholic culture to which Belloc belongs. At its best, Catholic society preserves the balance of the old paganism while introducing a new leaven of devotion. The truth of this is tacitly recognized by people who accuse the Catholic countries of worldliness and an unseemly gaiety. Belloc's work exhibits to the full the balanced joy in living of the humanist—a joy intensified by a Faith that makes all things, even the most trivial, significant because sacramental. And above all in his laughter, that levity of heart which is so irritating to those who do not understand its origin, we hear the authentic note of the Catholic humanist. The " good news " of Christmas brought an entirely new note of mirth into the world—a note that the pagan, with all his balanced joy in living, had lacked.

The humanistic basis of Catholic Christianity was brought out by Chesterton in his remark upon the choice of Peter as the foundation stone of the Faith. It was not, he said the mystical St. John, or the scholar, St. Luke, that Christ chose, but a shuffler, a liar, a snob, a coward: in a word, a *man* — a paradoxical way of expressing the truth that the Church was, from the start, built upon one of the most intensely human characters of all time. St. Peter, with his proletarian common sense, his large-hearted affection, his selfishness and fear for his own skin, and his potentiality for profound love and sacrifice, was the perfect example of an average human being. He was average not only in his character but in his occupation; and it is deeply significant that Our Lord likened his fishing boat to the Church afloat upon the stormy sea of the world. *Humanisme intégral* is the distinctive character of the great majority of Catholic saints in all ages and lands.

The Catholic middle ages, which gave to the world so many saints, have been praised for their deep spirituality; but what is most frequently overlooked is the intense humanism of all that time. Chaucer has mirrored it in verse—the colour, the pageantry, the gaiety, the emotional robustness and intellectual clarity, the strong passions and equally strong powers of renunciation. It was epitomized in the towering and multiform Gothic cathedral. Belloc, whose work has something of that Gothic multifariousness together with its humanistic unity of structure and spiritual aim, has often been called a mediaevalist; and in the best sense of the word, he is. Many people reject the word mediaevalist contemptuously as implying a backward-looking, unpractical mentality. But no living writer is more realistic and practical than Belloc. His mediaevalism is not of the romantic Victorian brand, but springs from his roots in the Faith. He would recall us to our origins; not to go back, but in order that we may once again go forward along the road we have lost—the ancient Roman road, pagan at its beginning, but gradually broadening out into a great Christian highway along which the humanists of the world have travelled. At one point on its journey this long road passes over a hill called Golgotha; and from that eminence of grief rises the stream of Christian mirth—a sublime paradox of which the key is to be found in the spirit of Belloc and of all who think and feel as he does.

I shall have something to say of Belloc's sociology in its proper place; but his "mediaevalism" recalls a charge very often brought against him. It is said, even by those who admire it theoretically, that his sociology would function admirably in the middle ages but is quite inapplicable to the industrial age. There is no doubt some truth in this criticism; but it is based upon a fallacy—the pragmatic fallacy that because an idea has become temporarily unworkable it is therefore wrong. The best in the mediaeval sociological scheme enshrined certain eternal truths: the evil of usury, the right of ownership and of responsibility towards other owners, and most of all, man's relation to the earth from which he sprang and the God by Whom he lives. The modern world has not only drifted away from these truths; it has slowly and with the inevitability of doom so hemmed itself round with error that it seems beyond salvation. But the fact that a man has, by wantonly neglecting his health, reached a stage almost past healing, does not invalidate the laws of health; and neither does the chaos of our mass-urban society with its vast cities, whose very size and structure inhibit the application of social truth, mean that those who reaffirm the laws of social health should be decried as archaic.

It is, however, easy to see why such social laws seem archaic to the modern world. We have travelled so far from the civilization they embody that our power of assimilating them has become atrophied. Everywhere, otherwise enlightened men, despairing of a way out of the modern chaos, with its mechanical intricacy, its economic stress, and scientific myopia, are crying out for more regimentation and planning—a remedy that only aggravates the disease; and the tragedy is that they are eagerly listened to by the multitude. As a solution of human evil they urge a course that would end in the destruction of human nature.

If we ask how the present impasse has come about, the answer is, I think, partly through the effects of the Reformation and the Renaissance. Each, in its different way, helped to destroy the humanistic spirit. The Reformation with its inwardness gravitated towards transcendentalism, while the worldliness that resulted from the Renaissance led to a growth of secularism and materialism. The fruits of the Reformation were Pietism, Kantianism, and finally Modernism which reduces the entire structure of Christianity to subjective need. The fruits of the Renaissance were Erastianism, exaggerated nationalism, and finally, *via* machinery, totalitarianism. Thus the two age old enemies of humanism, transcendentalism and materialism, arose once again.

Wilfred Wellock has pointed out how, from another aspect, the Reformation, as well as contributing to transcendentalism, also contributed obliquely to materialist dehumanization. It was " largely due to a fatal weakness in Non-conformity," which " arose from the view that the world, including human nature, is evil, and thus that spiritual well-being is to be found in God-man relationships only, never in human relationships." He adds that " in these circumstances, business life escaped the criticism of religion. Economics being divorced from ethics, greed ran riot . . ." Hence totalitarianism was bound to triumph, primarily through its own force (since it is centralized, organized and mechanized) and also through the oblique strength imparted to it, unwittingly, by idealistic Christianity.

And all this time the dim light of secular, and later, scientific humanism, has burned in cultural circles. But secular humanism cannot endure because, although it is well-intentioned, it lacks the grasp of the supernatural in human nature. It breeds a curious negative egoism, and with it a despair that falls an easy prey to positive totalitarian egoism. Today, although the kindly secular humanist is still found in odd corners of universities, the only effective challenge to totalitarianism is the humanism of the Catholic Church.

The Catholic Church stands as the chief bulwark against the inhuman mechanistic tendencies of the day—a fact that is clearly evident in the psychology of men produced by and living under the Catholic culture. Wherever the Faith has influence, and particularly in countries of the Latin culture, we shall find the humanistic spirit. The French are an intensely humanistic people, exemplifying in their approach to life, and in their thought and art, an abiding devotion to human ideals and interest in human affairs, which sometimes makes them appear superficial when contrasted with the mystical German or the imaginative Englishman.

I think we shall probably find a good deal of the explanation of Belloc's humanism in his French ancestry. He has been singularly happy in his heredity. Of good French stock on his father's side and the best type of English ancestry on his mother's, he has inherited the most admirable qualities of each nation: the Faith, the humanistic spirit, and economy and balance of style from France; imagination, lyrical power and verbal fecundity from England. The result—plus his own unique genius which, like all genius is unaccountable—is a remarkable blend of logic with inspiration in his thought, and strength with flexibility in his style. The most satisfying thing in his work at its best is the balance of what are normally opposing qualities. From one angle he is a too formal writer; yet it is equally possible to criticize him on the grounds of imaginative exuberance. His sense of form and innate common sense restrain his flights of imagination and lyricism, while these, in turn, take wing whenever the pedestrian force of logic becomes too heavy. When Belloc, with Gallic precision and economy of words, is analysing or describing an ideological situation, Belloc the heir of Chaucer and Shakespeare and Dickens will suddenly illumine it with a flight of imaginative intuition like a burst of song from an English hedgerow.

But although the French and English heredity is so happily blended in Belloc, he remains, I think, fundamentally English; and this is probably due to the added weight given in his upbringing in this country. The part played by environment in the formation of personality is often underestimated. A man having parents of different nationalities, say French and English, will almost certainly exhibit chiefly the characteristics of the parent in whose country he has been brought up. Such a man will not be, to use the jargon, " half French " and " half English," but " a third French and two-thirds English." We derive not from two sources, our parents, but from three, our parents and our environment; and experience, observation and psychology all point to the fact that environment plays the decisive part. The effect of English literature and institutions and, above all, the English countryside, acting upon heredity, have determined the predominantly English quality of Belloc's character and work. He recalls the best type of Chaucerian Englishman in the days when character was no less national for being part of a wider European culture; and we should not have looked far to find his prototype among that gay and gallant company who went singing down the road to Canterbury.

THE HISTORIAN

BY inclination and training Belloc is primarily an historian; and it is as an historian that I propose to consider him first. He began his career with a first-class honours degree in history at Oxford; and though he did not specialize in history, the historical spirit informs all his work. Because he has pursued his own way in his historical studies, and kept his mind open by discussing and writing about other subjects, he has developed a more sensitive view of history than many of his contemporaries. Furthermore, the fact that he is a man of artistic sensibility, has given him an intuitive understanding of history that complements his learning. He has brought a consistently historical viewpoint to all subjects—and rightly, since history informs all subjects; but he has not exclusively specialized in any branch of history and is therefore looked upon with suspicion in academic quarters. Yet he is no less a genuine historian because he has written successful essays, novels and verse.

Humanism and history are closely related. As Belloc himself has written: if the historian "be not seized of the mind which lay behind all that was human in the business then no synthesis of his detailed knowledge is possible." And again—" so far as truth is concerned it would be far better that a man should be possessed of no history than that he should be possessed of history ill-stated as to its prime factor, which is human motive."

But although history is principally the study of the acts of human personalities, it is frequently approached from the angle of metaphysics or science; or it may be confined to mere documentation. Hegel is an example of the meta-physical, Marx of the scientific historian. Hegel, like most romantic philosophers, was a secular theocentric, whereas Marx was primarily an economist. Both, however, were united in knowing very little about man. Similarly, the pedestrian research worker with his vast documentary know-ledge is often supremely ignorant of the motives of human nature. I am not decrying the work done by the philo-sophical, scientific and documentary historians: their work is essential, as a background. But they do not get to the psychological heart of history.

It so happens that where history is approached, as Belloc approaches it, primarily from the humanistic and psycho-logical angle, it is in the paradoxical position of being un-reliable as pure knowledge but satisfactory as charactero-logical intuition. Conversely, those who approach history from the scientific angle make it much more explicable as process, but by ignoring the essential human element, i.e., the characterological *interpretation* of process, tend to falsify the entire picture. Psychological history, as opposed to event history, is exposed to the charge of inaccuracy and bias, but it gets to the heart of things. The psychological judgments of the humanistic historian are not susceptible of proof: they cannot be measured or documented: they can only be grasped in the light of human experience.

Belloc's humanism, his love for and entirely unsentimental understanding of his fellow-men, impart to his historical writings the stamp of psychological truth. While in no way questioning his competence and accuracy in the scientific and documentary sphere, I would emphasize the dominant psychological character of his approach to history without which it cannot be properly understood. He has, I believe, been much influenced by Lingard, one of the most fair-minded and scientific of historians; but whatever the scientific standard of his historical work may be, it would, I submit, succeed by its psychological insight alone.

It is, of course, possible to approach history psychologically and yet fail to get to the heart of things. Many of our " official historians " (as Belloc calls them) fail in this way. They recognize the personal dynamic of historical events, but lacking the psychological acumen that proceeds from a genuine, innate humanism, they judge by behaviour rather than by intuition—probably as a result of approaching human nature in its superficial, external activity. The deep complicated wells of intention behind external behaviour are the province of the artist. Now Belloc is fortunate in possessing a profound artistic sensibility and insight into personality and character, and this has helped him enormously in his psychological approach to history. The relation and interplay of personalities is seen to be decisive in all his historical writings. The economic factor is interpreted mainly in the light of human greed, and the changing political scene and religious upheaval are attributed primarily to human folly and pride. Thus for Belloc the Reformation in England was largely due to the character of Anne Boleyn. It is significant that so very different a thinker as Bertrand Russell seems to subscribe to this view of history; and I recall some remark of his on the intimate relation of the first world war to the state of the health of a certain German official on a certain day. " For my part," says Russell, " I consider that whatever is good or bad is embodied in individuals, not primarily in communities."

There is another objection to psychological history, apart from inaccuracy and bias. If, it is argued, we find it difficult to judge the personality and motives of one whom we know intimately here and now, how can we judge a multitude of individuals, each with his own unique character and circumstances, who lived centuries ago under conditions totally different from our own ? We cannot, the philosophical and scientific historians reply: we can but record impersonal process; we must recognize our limitations, and avoid becoming entangled in psychological speculations that only serve to confuse historical fact.

The answer, which Belloc himself has given, is that the psychological perspective of events becomes clearer the farther the events recede. A humanist of genius, one possessing a deep psychological insight into the ways of men, is able to form sound judgments of character and motive if he knows what followed each action. Ordinarily we see both the individual and the crowd too closely in the contemporary scene: in history we see them and the world they created in perspective.

Belloc's method is to interpret historical process in the light of the characterological relations of individuals, whom he judges by means of his own wide and profound experience of life. Those of us who are at one with Belloc in his judgments of men, will best appreciate his historical work: these who are not, will appreciate it less. But the inhuman should avoid it, or they will be in a continual state of critical exasperation.

Belloc is sometimes accused of bias by those who are insensitive to his humanistic genius. If by bias they mean arguing forcibly for what a man believes to be true, they are simply stating a fact. But they do not mean this. They mean that Belloc tends to mould history to suit his own preconceived notions. Now in my experience, this accusation of bias is usually brought forward by men themselves plainly biased in the opposite direction. This fact does not, of course, answer the charge of bias: a thief can catch a thief. But it certainly weakens it. In the main it is probable that much of the criticism of Belloc on this score has come from the unfamiliarity of his position. The charge is less frequently made to-day, when many have come much closer to Belloc's position, than it was some years ago. Perhaps the chief cause of the charge of bias (apart from the universal human desire for belittlement) is the clarity and force of his judgments together with an, at times, rather pontifical manner. At his worst, Belloc can be irritatingly dogmatic, and this often obscures the soundness of his judgment and the logic of his reasoning. Furthermore, accentuation of the personal element in his historical work often heightens the effect of partisanship.

Thus the humanism of Belloc is at once his strength and his weakness as an historian. His strength in the insight into character it gives him, and his weakness in the partisan tendencies (inseparable from all problems of human relationship) it generates. But the deep insight into character far outweighs any partisan tendencies.

Belloc is a realist. He avoids sentimental adulation, and angry vilification; and I know of no single case in which his treatment of an historical character is marred by these characteristics. Realism is a quality of genuine humanism. The idealist tends to see men in terms of the future, as they ought to be in ethical or metaphysical theory; the scientist tends to see men as they behave in terms of the past, as the products of biological causation; but the humanist sees men as they are, because he thinks and feels at one with them. When humanism is the *humanisme intégral* of the living Faith, realism is reinforced by knowledge of the supernatural origins of human nature—an attitude which explains the Christian saints who were both lovers and cynics. They knew men: they were not deceived by them: but at the same time they loved every individual because every individual is made in the image of God. The transcendentalist idealizes men; the materialist usually despises him; but only the Christian humanist can combine worldly cynicism and spiritual devotion—a fact that explains Belloc's synthesis of sensibility and irony in the delineation of character. If we would get the best out of Belloc's historical work, we must concentrate on the interplay of character rather than on documentation and analysis of events.

Another advantage of the psychological or humanistic approach to history is that it makes the past *live*. What is called, for want of a better word, academic history, rarely lives. The facts are there, and they are often expressed with scholarly beauty and restraint of language; but there is no vision, no communication of emotion to the reader in such a way that he grasps the historical situation as though he were himself a living part of it. Whether or no we accept Belloc's interpretation of history, we must admit that he does succeed in communicating the past to us so vividly that we seem to re-live it. And this power is assuredly the reason for his growing influence—in spite of academic prejudice and neglect. The psychological interpretation of history may be, at times, incomplete and over-personal; but I submit that it gives us, on the whole, a closer approximation to the truth that lies at the heart of things than metaphysics or science.

Apart from character, which is decisive, there is another field in which Belloc excels in the writing of history: the description of military manoeuvres and battles. He possesses a wide theoretical and practical knowledge of military matters. He served his term as a conscript in the French army (he was born on French soil) and contributed a remarkable series of war commentaries to the periodical *Land and Water* during the first world war. Under his hand, the dullest of old battles and manoeuvres glow with life, and he can make the most complicated military situation clear. Battles, though their influence is over-rated, play a major part in history, and not the least of Belloc's historical gifts is his military knowledge.

To evaluate Belloc's complete historical effort would be impossible here. It is, like his work in other fields, rather unequal; but at its best it is the best of Belloc. Roughly, it falls into three groups. The first comprises works of English history, the second, works of French history, and the third, works dealing with history in general. Some are technical in form, but a very large number are biographies, as we should expect. His contributions to English history are, however, his principal effort in the historical field. The *History of England* (in 4 volumes, unfinished) is an astonishing achievement for a man who has written so much and in so many fields. It moves forward with an intellectual vitality and a verbal clarity and strength that bear the impress of genuine greatness; and it may come to be regarded as the most psychologically penetrating history of the Englishman and his institutions that exists.

The *Shorter History* in one volume is also a fine achievement. It is in some ways more difficult to write a good short history than to produce a detailed work with its greater comprehensiveness and easier scope for development. The perennial literary problem of avoiding both understatement and verbosity is intensified in a short history, in which the commonest defects are a synopsis-like compression, or the over-development of some period, character, or event that seems to the writer important, at the expense of balance and proportion. It is very easy to lose the sense of proportion in this kind of work and thus destroy the panoramic effect of the whole. On the whole Belloc has succeeded in avoiding these defects, although it might be argued that he has given too much space to the Irish Famine and its repercussions. History, even of one's own country, is so vast a subject, that for the student (and this work is intended mainly for students) it is best taken broadly, since it enables him to experience the *movement* of events. Just as on a hill we look down at a train passing through the valley below, and in that broad perspective see its motion and direction as we never could close up to the line, so, in a good short history, we grasp something of the historical process as a moving whole. Belloc is admirably fitted to produce a successful short history in which his great gifts of logic, sensibility, psychological insight, and economical yet comprehensive statement can be exploited to the full. The great characters and events of the past emerge from the *Shorter History* with unparalleled force and vividness.

Among the historico-biographical studies (which many believe are his masterpieces) those of *Charles I* and *Cromwell* are outstanding and typical; and some of the most remarkable examples of his fertility and resource are to be found in his treatment of the same events in these two books. Though covering so much of the same ground there is no sterile repetition. *Charles I* is a tragedy; *Cromwell* has an epic quality.

In the study of Charles the forces that brought the king to his death move forward with the inevitability of doom, and the prose is of a sustained majesty and power unsurpassed anywhere by its author. The character of Charles is analysed with sympathy, but with a detachment that entirely rules out the sentimentality so often associated with him.

> I may compare the effects of his inward strength to the effects produced by one kind of resistance against an impact.
>
> When men plan to make impact against resistance in the will of another they expect, and commonly find, at first a resistance. They proceed to wear it down. If it gets less, they are introduced to a last struggle in which, when they have taken all the outworks they may naturally expect to succeed. So it was with the pressure brought against the boy's father, James I, in the first beginnings of the revolt of the gentry against him. James's Parliaments—that is is, the country gentlemen—pushed him further and further. Such an action is like a siege, it can have but one end, and as we know, James, fighting from trench to trench, always, in the end, gave way.
>
> Then again, there is the kind of resistance offered by men who are adamant from the beginning. They bluntly refuse, and if you lose your first battle against them you can go no further.
>
> But Charles was to be neither of these. His nature, trained in isolation, was fluid against the first onset of attack; then there came a moment when the attack reached something quite different from the first fluid resistance—a stone wall. It was thus that he came to his death. Men were led on to think him pliable; when they came unexpectedly on rigidity, they were infuriated.
>
> Now this distinction, I take it, between his fixity upon certain things, well defined in his own mind, and his indecision or rather lack of convinced *cause* for resistance on the rest—this quality in him which kept in reserve and hidden an ultimate power of complete refusal (even to martyrdom) took root, I say, in these very early years when he was compelled, almost against himself, to consider in private what remedy he could find for his defects.

This judgment bears the stamp of psychological truth, as do those of Buckingham, Pym, Laud, and other great figures that emerge from the book. I suggest that anyone who would grasp the essential Belloc should acquaint himself with this book and its companion, *Cromwell*. In the former, Belloc concentrates mainly upon the characters of the king and of the men around him, with the effect of high tragedy (for tragedy proceeds from the clash of personal-

ities); in the latter, he deals more with impersonal movements, with the battles of the Civil War and the economic
movements of the age (without ever losing sight of the
central figure), and it is this that gives the book its epic
quality.

But it seems to me that in *Cromwell*, Belloc makes one of
his rare psychological blunders. Buchan, in his study of the
Protector, argues that he had no prior intention of killing the
king or of overthrowing parliament, but that circumstances
forced it upon him at the last moment, while Belloc believes
that he had planned his work of destruction for some time.
Surely the truth lies between these two extremes. It is more
probably that Cromwell was an example of what St.
Augustine called " the dual will," that which we recognize
to-day as the source of neurotic conflict. It seems that he
argued consciously towards the good, while all the time
moving subconsciously towards power—a process that in a
simpler age men would have called self-deception. He
argued consciously for the salvation of the king, while the
hidden purpose of his dynamic subconscious worked for
Charles' destruction. Nevertheless, the rather insensitive
view of Cromwell which Belloc advances is offset by some
astonishing flashes of insight into his tortured and enig-
matical character.

The studies of French history are centred mainly in the
great figures of the French Revolution: Robespierre,
Danton, Marie Antoinette. That which appeals to Belloc
in the Revolution is its insistence on the rights of *man*.

One of his commonest failings in the historical sphere is
a tendency to the over-simplification of impersonal issues.
In dealing with character he rarely over-simplifies; but he is
inclined to reduce complicated, impersonal events to one
or two fundamental formulae which, though significant in
themselves, tend to give a one-sided picture of things. Thus
in my view he exaggerates the influence of the money power,
and this leads him, at times, to very incomplete general-
ization about the class that wielded that power. Money was
a powerful force, but only one of a number of forces that
brought about the modern world. The strange thing is that
Belloc seems to be unaware of the fact that his vividly

truthful psychological portraits often disharmonize with his limited conception of their economic background.

Something of this over-simplification (and we must remember that it also leads to the charge of bias) is to be found in *Europe and the Faith*. " Europe is the faith, and the faith is Europe " Belloc tells us. It is a profound truth; and it is also a vast simplification. But *Europe and the Faith* is a great book because it reveals Belloc's profound sense of Europe. He is at once the most insular of men and the most cosmopolitan: his love of Sussex is the nucleus of his love of Europe, of the Faith and of all mankind. As a humanist of deep sensibility and understanding, as one whose heredity has given him a sense of Europe almost unique among modern Englishmen, and as an heir to the Faith that created Europe, Belloc is supremely well equipped for the writing of history. All his writings are informed by an innate, all-pervading historical sense. History, he has himself told us, is his greatest interest. It is also, we may add, his greatest achievement.

THE SOCIOLOGIST

HISTORY may be described as the sociology of the past: sociology is history in the present. This is, of course, a simplification; but it is roughly true. All sociology must plan ahead, but its primary function is the diagnosis of the present in terms of past experience. It follows that the most effective sociology is based upon psychological history, which is concerned with the needs and aims of men. The majority of our sociological thinkers to-day are tainted with exactly the same weakness as we discovered in the historians, and for the same reason; they tend to approach sociology either too metaphysically or too scientifically. Thus we see the same forces acting upon the whole of life—the ceaseless drag of idealism and materialism away from the concrete unity of individual personality. We have considered their effects in general in relation to the broad principles of humanism; and also to history. But the dangers of inhuman abstractionism, whether idealist or materialist, in sociology are incalculable. Much is made of the opiate of religion, whereas the real danger to human life to-day is the utopiate of abstract sociology.

A humanistic sociology is the heir of a humanistic reading of history which, in turn, derives from a humanistic view of life. Now Belloc's Catholic humanism, which has so admirably fitted him for the task of understanding the deeper psychological processes of history, has also enabled him to diagnose accurately the sociological problems of the present. In his sociological writings we shall find the most explicit expression of his Catholic humanism. We shall see him re-affirming again and again in different contexts the sacredness of individual personality and the right to evenly-distributed property; the necessity of regionalism in government; the family, the parish and the guild as the fundamental social unit; the return to a healthy agricultural policy, to the land, and to the Faith that made Europe and can alone safeguard the human sanities that make life worth living. In his reading of English history he traces the development of the forces that have destroyed these things: in his sociology he applies his reading of history to the problem of restoring them. Both are complementary.

The broad name for the sociological movement which Belloc, and, with him, Chesterton and a small but influential group of followers helped to found, is *distributism*. Its basic maxim is " the restoration of liberty through the distribution of property "; and its inspiration is Belloc's *The Servile State*—a book as terse and as dynamic as Rousseau's *Social Contract*. The humanistic character of distributism is so bound up with Belloc's life and work that I must define it in some detail.

The sociological groupings of the modern world seem to be broadly four in number: capitalism, socialism, anarchism and distributism. Capitalism comprises a large number of related systems, all depending, in the last resort, upon the control of power by rich men, more or less independent of the state. Under socialism can be grouped marxism, fabianism, and various forms of fascism, all depending in the last resort upon the control of power by a dictator or a bureaucratic committee, calling himself or themselves, the State. Both capitalism and socialism tend to unite in *totalitarianism*. Anarchism is comparatively isolated. It contains elements of socialism and distributism; but though its ideal is sound it cannot establish itself without seizing the state, and thereby destroying its own principles. Distributism has something in common with anarchism, but inter-penetrates all sociologies to some extent while retaining a distinct psychological character of its own. Capitalism, socialism and anarchism, however, have one thing in common: they have to be *imposed* upon society.

Capitalism is unintellectual, and has never been for-mulated with precision. It is based mainly upon *laissez-faire* and greed, and is imposed by tacit coercion, political and legal. Conversely, socialism in all its forms is predominently intellectual and systematized—even the anti-intellectual elements of some forms of fascist socialism are, ironically, intellectual in content, a kind of philosophical *nihilism*. Socialism is theoretically based upon the idea of equality, but practically upon dictatorial or bureaucratic power, and is imposed by force of arms, by revolution, or by persuasion. Anarchism, no less intellectual, is actively hostile to the capitalist and socialist centralization of power, and although based upon the ideal of universal freedom, can only be imposed by terrorism. Distributism differs from each of these systems in that it has not to be imposed upon society, but is itself the ground of society. It does not come into being: it *is;* and all that distributists can do is to enlarge the scope of an already existent world-principle. Distributism rejects both capitalist materialism and socialist utopianism. It is concrete and humanistic, and is based upon the funda-mental psychological needs of mankind.

The humanistic basis of distributism is the reason for its adaptability and flexibility. Thus a distributist-industrialist society may contain capitalist and socialist elements: there may be some excess of wealth and some poverty side by side with a certain amount of state ownership—banks, postage, mines, etc. Or again, a distributist-rural society may be anarchistic in form—that is, decentralized and equalitarian with, in some cases, the members of different farms sharing their labour and implements. But a distributist society will always and everywhere be *distributist*, i.e., ownership, and with it the sense of freedom and responsibility that ownership confers will, in Belloc's words, be " the dominant note of that society." This adaptability of distributism explains why it was possible for pre-1940 France to be distributist while under a corrupt democracy, and a country like Portugal to be distributist while under a benevolent autocracy. It explains the presence of distributive elements in socialist countries such as Russia, and capitalist countries such as England and America. In England the small farmers and shopkeepers are still the most vital representatives of their race. Nor should we forget the vast rural-distributive systems of India and China; for although distributism is intimately bound up with Christianity, in essence it is as old as man.

The humanistic spirit explains the permanence, endurance and strength of distributism. It is not centred in competitive economics, nor in philosophy and science, nor in abstract ethics: it is centred in the psychological needs of the human spirit. It does not systematize: it synthesizes. It is not imposed: it grows. Nevertheless, distributism is in very great danger of being swept from great parts of the earth to-day, a danger that Belloc analysed and forecast so brilliantly in *The Servile State*. The work has become a classic, and is a microcosm of Belloc's entire sociological outlook.

The thesis of *The Servile State* reveals the unity of Belloc's history and sociology, and the Catholic humanism which is the source of that unity. He begins with a short historical survey which suffers from some of the over-simplification discussed above but has the ring of truth. In the England of the early 16th century, he tells us, the Church was lord over nearly 30 per cent. of the agricultural communities; but the action of Henry VIII (in confiscating the monastic lands, apart from about 10 per cent. which remained in the hands of the secular clergy) at one stroke placed 20 per cent. of the nation's wealth in the hands of the Crown. Belloc here suggests that had the Crown—as Henry originally

intended—retained the monopoly of the land looted from
the Church, the new capitalist state might never have come
into being, and instead a strong monarchy on the lines of
France would probably have arisen. But, he adds, the
large landowners who already controlled a quarter to a
third of the agricultural wealth, were too strong, and insisted
on land grants from the Crown, many of them by way of
payment for their assistance in obtaining the loot; and in
this way they added, to the third they already owned, a
fifth of the total wealth and became possessed of nearly half
the land. He then goes on to point out how the possession
of this wealth operated on the social structure: how the
new rich began to dominate parliament and to fill the
universities and legal profession, and how the Crown was
further weakened and impoverished under the reigns of
a sickly boy and two women. By the time of James I, the
power of the rich had grown to such an extent that the
Crown was virtually at their mercy.

Here the close relation of Belloc's historical and sociological outlook is clearly revealed. The forces that weakened the Catholic Church and atrophied the Crown ended
by destroying freedom and ownership, and gave us capitalism, the nucleus of the Servile State. It would, I suggest,
greatly help towards the understanding of *The Servile State*
to read the studies *Elizabethan Commentary*, *Charles I*,
Cromwell, and *The Last Rally* as background, since these
volumes work out in detail the historical basis of the
sociological treatise.

Now it is central to Belloc's argument (and to the Catholic
viewpoint as expressed in the Papal Encyclicals) that not
only capitalism, but its proposed remedy, socialism, tends
equally to the production of servility. Capitalism puts
wealth into the hands of a few rich men, while socialism,
the supposed remedy for capitalism, puts the power repre-
sented by the wealth into the hands of state officials—a
much more dangerous form of tyranny. Thus plutocracy
gives way to bureaucracy. " The effect of Socialist doctrine
upon Capitalist society, is to produce a third thing—to
wit, the Servile State." Belloc characteristically brings this
home by the metaphor of a traveller who, desirous of leaving

the cold of the mountains for the warmer south, begins to follow a river that appears to be going southward. But one knowing the mountans better points out that the river does not go southward at all, and that by following it the traveller will find himself north again. " The traveller is the Socialist. The South which he desires to reach is the Collectivist State. The River is modern ' Organized Reform.' The Northern country where the mountain river will ultimately find a quiet bed is a society reposing upon compulsory labour." And—he might have added—the man who knows the mountains and points out the error is the humanst, while the river is the stream of history. Belloc is a master in the use of exact and picturesque metaphor, as this example reveals: instead of going off into a maze of abstraction, he will follow a logical argument by an imaginative picture.

The Servile State, written in 1912, is a remarkable instance of Belloc's foresight. Many of its predictions have been fulfilled in the contemporary world. But his ability to forecast has nothing in common with the timeless vision of the mystical seer: it proceeds from a sound, earthly judgment derived from an intuitive humanism—a feeling for the way men behave. In this connexion, it is interesting to contrast Belloc's prophetic insight with that of Marx. Marx's unpsychological mind was insensitive to the levelling tendency of the middle class which did not fit in to his abstract, ideological scheme. He was quite unable to shake free from the economic myth of his beautifully constructed system; hence he prophesied proletarian revolution. Belloc, the humanist, observing his fellow man, feeling with him and entering into his life, foresaw the growth of the Servile State as partly produced, and implicity acquiesced in, by the growing middle class. This was in 1912. Within 30 years totalitarianism, the apotheosis of the Servile State in all its forms, had begun to establish itself in almost every part of the globe—and, most ironically, the wars that were fought against its dangerous tendencies only served to strengthen it. Nowhere did we witness the dynamic proletarian revolution prophesied by Marx. Even in Russia, where conditions were most favourable, the so-called popular revolution was not a spontaneous movement, but was imposed from above upon a chaotic situation by a handful of bourgeois philosophers, the majority of whom had never done a day's proletarian work in their lives. Everywhere, as Belloc had forecast, the people tamely acquiesced in their slavery, and accepted the dictators and bureaucrats. He saw the coming of the sinister Labour Camp—as when he wrote in *The Servile State:* " The Labour Colony (a prison so-called because euphemism is necessary to every transition) will be erected to absorb this surplus, and that last form of compulsion will crown the edifice of these reforms."

Totalitarianism has proved beyond any doubt that all forms of materialism are inhuman. It was easy enough for the cloistered scientist and economist of a generation ago to work out their abstract schemes for the betterment of mankind on a non-supernatural basis, for the simple reason that a materialistic society had never been tried. To such men the shortcomings of Christian society in its long 2,000 years' history was only too obvious. It was quite easy to discredit Christianity which everybody had experienced, and to contrast it with a materialistic society which nobody had experienced. When, however, materialism emerged from the common room and study into crude social practice, the old academic materialism received a violent blow. Here was the practical result of its teaching: revolution, persecution, tyranny, war: a nightmare world.

What we now easily deduce after the fact, Belloc foresaw long before the fact. *The Servile State* must have seemed a merely alarmist piece of work to many in the serene days of 1912; and not only alarmist, but fundamentally wrong headed in its forecast that socialism, the great hope of the intellectuals, would turn out to be the reverse side of the capitalist medal. But to-day we see that the main drift of Belloc's thought was right. Making due allowance for over-simplification, it is broadly true that the totalitarian servile state is the logical consequence of the break-up of the Faith in the 16th century.

On Christian premises, man is a psychophysical unit of spirit and matter, and any sociology that rejects the supernatural is bogus. But on materialist premises, the logic of totalitarianism is unanswerable. Man, the materialist argues, partly through economic greed, and partly through adherence to the illusions of religion, has grossly over-stressed individual personality, and the result has been muddle, incompetence, distortion and injustice. Re-organized on the lines of the *hymenoptera* he will go forward into a new world of dynamic, impersonal order, based upon the great scientific conception of energy. Struggle is the law of life by which the strongest nation or class succeeds and dominates; and revolution and war are the forces by which the dynamic groups will ultimately be brought to form one world-pattern, religionless, classless and ultimately human-less. That is the menacing logic of materialist totali-tarianism, whatever form it may take.

But in spite of this insane doctrine, man remains, above all, an individual—a *person;* and the trend of human evolution towards a greater and deeper integration of personality cannot be permanently opposed. World-totalitarianism can never be completely realized; and though slavery may last in many parts of the earth for generations, it must ultimately break—since the application of pressure to a community destroys the system that applies it as surely as the forcing of steam into a closed container. Without the safety valve of personal initiative, repressed human individuality will explode and blow the social structure to pieces. World-totalitarianism must be followed by world-anarchy.

For Belloc the tragedy is that we are acquiescing in the slow destruction of our liberties; and it is cold comfort to know that a totalitarian world cannot permanently endure. The one answer to the inhuman totalitarian slave state is the *humanisme intégral* of which Catholic Christianity is the fount and head—a humanism that expresses itself in the distribution of property and personal responsibility, the family, the earth-life in harmony with nature, and the universal Church, Christ begotten, and Christ centred.

Like most of Belloc's ideological works, *The Servile State* is chiefly effective as a broad survey. Though undeniably a logical thinker, Belloc is not, on the whole, a detailed thinker: his best work is distinguished by a virile grasp of essentials to the exclusion of analysis and detail. In many cases this is a virtue; but occasionally the simplicity of his logic and neglect of dialectical detail can be the cause of confusion, as in his very incomplete treatment of the problem of freedom and happiness. In the Preface to the second edition he writes of certain misconceptions that have arisen in connexion with the word "servile". "It is" he says, " as though I had used the word in some rhetorical sense of ' irksome ' or ' oppressive,' whereas I have attempted to use it only under the limits of my definition "—that is as compulsory labour. All the same, he does appear to use it in the former sense. In Chapter I he says that slavery is "irksome, undignified, woeful," but as though remembering his disclaimer, he adds, a couple of paragraphs later, that " men (are) happy in that arrangement, or, at least, as happy as men ever are." Now to say that under a smooth-working totalitarian state, men are " as happy as men ever are " is to imply that men will not be happier under any other system. Clearly there is either some implicit subtlety, or a contradiction here. This obscurity is unfortunate, since the word servile is not only the main word of Belloc's title, but the key word to his thesis. Belloc has given a false impression by his refusal to face the necessity for dialectical subtlety in this kind of writing. Such subtleties are foreign to his mind, and he doubtless considers that they would obscure the broad lines of his thesis as a whole; but they are essential to the argument.

Whatever happens in the world at large, Belloc is very doubtful if distributism will return to modern England. But just enough of the old free spirit remains to justify him in formulating a plan for improvement. Hence in 1936, twenty-four years after the publication of *The Servile State*, he published what might be regarded as a sequel to it: *An Essay on the Restoration of Property*. It is a close, concise statement of the problems attendant upon the restoration of property in capitalist England, and of the methods by which such a restoration might be brought about. *The Servile State* is an analysis and a forecast; the *Essay* is a plan of action. Various proposals are put forward, such as differential taxation in order to level wealth as much as possible; the subsidizing of small owners, and especially of those desirous of living on the land; the making law of equitable measures to prevent the development of combines, chain-stores and the like. But, with characteristic humanism, Belloc insists that there can be no improvement without the desire for property, freedom, and responsibility in the average man. Without the right psychological attitude, progress towards distributism is impossible. We have become accustomed to think of ourselves, not as productive owners, but as wage earners; and it is our false psychological attitude that daily strengthens the Servile State:

> The second proviso, that we can do nothing unless there is a state of mind favourable to us, may seem to make the whole effort futile. The state of society in which we are now living in England has largely forgotten what property is. Men talk in terms of employment and wages. When they talk of ownership the word calls up in their minds the ownership of large property by a few. Whether there remains to-day in England a desire for economic freedom (that is, for property) sufficient to nourish the beginnings of a change, nothing but experiment can decide. Increase of revenue, not ownership, is the object of most men.

It is typical of Belloc that he never allows his sense of the realities of human nature to be obscured by his sociological ideals. His sociological writings are distinguished for their psychological insight, realism, and complete honesty in following wherever the conclusion leads, and for their clarity and force of utterance. His ideal is a Christian distributist society, multiform and fertile, wherein the note of government will be the safeguarding of property within such limits as allow the greatest liberty for each individual to develop his personality without encroaching upon the rights of his neighbour.

THE ESSAYIST

APART from his historical and sociological works Belloc has produced a large number of essays and miscellaneous writings. They can be broadly divided into Essays proper (such as the *On* series), Travel and

Topography, Literary Criticism, Fiction, Satire and Humour (including such pieces as *Mrs. Markham's History*) and Controversy.

All these miscellaneous writings cannot be fully understood apart from Belloc's history and sociology of which they are an overflow. Always, whether in pugnacious controversy or in his gayest and most inconsequential bits of work, we can trace the outlook of the man who wrote the *History of England* and *The Servile State;* in fact it is the view of life embodied in such writings that makes the irony and humour of the essays and miscellaneous writings convincing—so much so that, apart from the obvious satisfaction of the prose, people who do not appreciate the historian and sociologist will not get the best out of the other works.

Of the essay proper, in the more traditional and formal sense of the word, Belloc has given us many fine examples. (I mean, of course, the short essay of the type for which Lamb and to a lesser degree E. V. Lucas were masters.) This type of essay is a peculiarly humanistic form of expression: it is concrete, imaginative, vivid, observational, and, above all, centred in persons. Belloc's history and sociology reveal his psychological understanding of the ways and needs of men; his short essays reveal the warmth of his affection, and his charm. The human situation is the very essence of this form of writing, and there are no more companionable books than Belloc's numerous collection of essays such as the *On* series (*On Nothing*, *On Something*, *On Anything*, etc.) or *Hills and the Sea*. They reveal a consistently high level of writing and construction, from the earliest *On* books to the last collection entitled *Places*.

The *On* series, written about thirty years ago, contain some of the most glorious fooling and satire in the language. The note is struck in the exuberant dedication to Maurice Baring with which *On Nothing* opens:

> It was in Normandy, you will remember, and in the heat of the year, when the birds were silent in the trees and the apples nearly ripe, with the sun above us already of a stronger kind, and a somnolence within and without, that it was determined among us (the jolly company!) that I should write upon Nothing, and upon all that is cognate to Nothing, a task not yet attempted since the Beginning of the World.

Now when the matter was begun and the subject nearly approached, I saw more clearly that this writing upon Nothing might be very grave, and as I looked at it in every way, the difficulties of my adventure appalled me, nor am I certain that I have overcome them all. But I had promised you that I would proceed, and so I did, in spite of my doubts and terrors.

For first I perceived that in writing upon this matter I was in peril of offending the privilege of others, and of those especially who are powerful to-day, since I would be discussing things very dear and domestic to my fellow-men, such as The Honour of Politicians, The Tact of Great Ladies, The Wealth of Journalists, The Enthusiasm of Gentlemen, and the Wit of Bankers. All that is most intimate and dearest to the men that make our time, all that they would most defend from the vulgar gaze—this it was proposed to make the theme of a common book.

In spite of such natural fear and of interests so powerful to detain me, I have completed my task, and I will confess that as it grew it enthralled me. There is in Nothing something so majestic and so high that it is a fascination and spell to regard it. Is it not that which Mankind, after the great effort of life, at last attains, and that which alone can satisfy mankind's desire? Is it not that which is the end of so many generations of analysis, the final word of philosophy, and the goal of the search for reality? Is it not the very matter of our modern creed in which the great spirits of our time repose, and is it not, as it were, the culmination of their intelligence? It is indeed the sum and meaning of all round!

Although *Places* is not a vintage Belloc, it reveals as always his lucid style, balanced construction, sense of climax, and feeling for exactly the right length. (I would note in passing that his delight in places is largely determined by their human associations.) But one of the things we miss in *Places*, and in much of Belloc's latest work, is the humour and horse-play that characterized his earlier writings. There are signs that Belloc is tired—though the old humour is never entirely absent.

Belloc's humour is a very characteristic thing, and is intimately bound up with his outlook and temperament. It is often ironical, but without bitterness—for bitterness proceeds from frustrated idealism. The humanist, though he may attack his fellow men, attacks because he loves; not like Swift because he despairs. Belloc's irony is a blend of Gallic wit and English robustness. His love of sheer horse-play is very English: at its best, exhilarating; at its worst, irritating. But in one sense it reveals his humility, for he is fond of parodying his own dogmatism to a point of absurdity—a fact often overlooked by those who accuse him of saying clever things for the sake of effect. His humour, like all great humour, is at times very near to sorrow; but he is never sentimental. In all the great mass of his writings I do not believe it possible to detect a single sentimental passage.

Humour is closely bound up with the humanist outlook: the inhuman man, whether an idealist or a materialist, is usually humourless. The Christian humanist laughs at the world because he sees it as it is; the idealist mourns and the materialist rages because they wish it to be what it is not. One of the most terrifying things about totalitarianism is its blank humourlessness: the humourlessness of the machine. Somewhere Aldous Huxley remarks of one of his characters who becomes a Catholic that, like so many converts, he took to writing humorous verse. It is what we should expect.

All genuine humour is of its essence man-centred. Humour may be described, biologically, as a shock to the nervous system, communicating a reflex of sharp mental excitement; or psychologically—and more accurately—as a sudden perception of fortuitousness in the solemn order of human affairs. All humour is human, from the most brilliant satire to the spectacle of an elderly gentleman sitting on his hat; that is why fiction and the essay are such admirable vehicles for humour. Pictorial art, in the form of caricature, is capable of arousing humour: but as we proceed further away from the human towards the abstract and ideal, humour becomes less and less possible, until we reach music, an art as remote as mathematics. Music is almost totally humourless; and the one piece of music I know that has ever aroused laughter in a concert hall is Walton's *Facade*— a unique achievement. Humour has no part in heaven where all is perfect, or in hell where all is chaos; neither has it any part in philosophy and science where all is abstract. It proceeds essentially from the incongruousness of human life; from the fallen and therefore contradictory nature of man. It is not an exaggeration to say that the Fall of Man was the origin of humour. The Missal contains these significant words: "Oh blessed fault that brought the Redeemer into the world;" and that stupendous event of redemption inspired the joy of the Middle Ages and has conserved such laughter as remains in our dark industrial world.

Belloc has poked fun at most things; but he is sometimes rather insensitive to the feelings of the targets of his humour, particularly so in the case of the Jews. We must however, remember that he has also satirized politicians, imperialists, atheists, Protestants and Catholics.

Although Belloc has satirized his fellow Catholics, no one would deny his deep personal devotion. But his attitude to the Faith is not as much "devotional" as logical, social, objective. This logical, social, objective attitude to the world is, as we have seen, everywhere characteristic of humanism in whatever form. Humanism is psychological in character; logical in application. In *The Path to Rome*, during the course of that remarkable journey, Belloc tells how he heard Mass at a little village church: he stood throughout (as is customary with many on the continent) and observed with great reverence all that was going on. A momentary glimpse; yet it gives us the worldly, humanistic, but no less religious savour of the man. *The Path to Rome* is a classic: a great book which may be equalled but is not surpassed by Belloc for its inspired, vivid observation and description, and brilliant comment upon men and things. It is decorated with sketches by the author, which give us reason to believe that he would have done as well with the pencil as the pen if his versatile genius had led him that way. But among the miscellaneous writings I would single out for detailed comment *The Four Men*, since it is not only a great book but a microcosm of Belloc's entire outlook.

The intimate appeal of *The Four Men* derives from its enshrinement of an essentially human problem—the problem of the conflict between our sense of physical kinship with the earth and of spiritual kinship with God. It epitomizes Belloc's outlook, not explicitly as worked out in the movements of history and sociology, but implicitly, as a vision of life enshrined in the realm of human feeling and emotion. The setting is Sussex, and the

time October, " season of mists and mellow fruitfulness."
It is the eve of All Hallows, the hour of mystery, when the
English landscape is seen at its best, and every leaf is full
of mortality and the spirit of things past. Although it is
not apparent at first, the theme of All Hallows, when the
dead awaken—that strange festival, half pagan, half
Christian, which embodies in itself the conflict between
earthly loss and spiritual hope—is central to the message of
the whole work.

On the evening of October 29th, 1902, Myself, the
narrator, is " sitting in ' The George ' at Robertsbridge
drinking that port of their's," when, speaking his thoughts
aloud, he is answered by a tall, bearded stranger, Grizzlebeard, also of the county. They agree to journey together
from east to west, " to Arun, and the things we knew," and
at once the atmosphere of a spiritual adventure, a pilgrimage
of the soul, is set. Nothing explicit is said; but the sense of
distance and of far horizons is conveyed in every word. " To
Arun, and the things we knew." At the beginning of the
journey, Myself and Grizzlebeard, fall in with The Sailor
and The Poet also journeying westward; and together the
four men take their way over the high downs, through little
woods known only to the wise, through Bramber and
Steyning and Amberley, singing, versifying, telling tales,
arguing, quarrelling, and laughing as they go, until at last,
five days later on November 22nd, they came to South
Harting, " the end of all the county." Here in the mists of
a November dawn Grizzlebeard, The Sailor, and The Poet
part from Myself, who sees them, not as mortal men, but
as archtypes of the human spirit.

Then Myself sadly, remembering all the joys vouchsafed
on the memorable journey, goes eastwards back over the
Downs. His meditations are enshrined in one of the
greatest passages in English literature.

> I went up in gloom, by the nearest spur, on to the grass and
> into the loneliness of the high Downs that are my brothers and
> my repose; and, once upon their crest, setting my face eastward I
> walked on in a fever for many hours back towards the places from
> which we had come; and below me as I went was that good land-
> scape in which I had passed such rare and memorable hours.
>
> I still went on, through little spinneys here and there, and across

the great wave tops and rolls of the hills, and as the day proceeded and the light declined about me I still went on, now dipping into the gaps where tracks and roads ran over the chain, now passing for a little space into tall and silent woods wherever these might stand. And all the while I came nearer and nearer to an appointed spot of which a memory had been fixed for years in my mind. But as I strode, with such a goal in view, an increasing loneliness oppressed me, and the air of loss and the echo of those profound thoughts which had filled the last words we four had exchanged together.

It was in the grove above Lavington, near the mounds where they say old kings are buried, that I, still following the crest of my hills, felt the full culmination of all the twenty tides of mutability which had thus run together to make a skerry in my soul. I saw and apprehended, as a man sees or touches a physical thing, that nothing of our sort remains, and that even before my county should cease to be itself I should have left it. I recognized that I was (and I confessed) in that attitude of the mind wherein men admit mortality; something had already passed from me—I mean that fresh and vigorous morning of the eyes wherein the beauty of this land had been reflected as in a tiny mirror of burnished silver. Youth was gone out apart; it was loved and regretted, and therefore no longer possessed.

Then, as I walked through this wood more slowly, pushing before me great billows of dead leaves, as the bows of a ship push the dark water before them, this side and that, when the wind blows full on the middle of the sail and the water answers loudly as the ship sails on, so I went till suddenly I remembered with the pang that catches men at the clang of bells what this time was in November; it was the Day of the Dead. All that day I had so moved and thought alone and fasting, and now the light was falling. I had consumed the day in that deep wandering on the heights alone, and now it was evening. Just at that moment of memory I looked up and saw that I was there. I had come upon the lawn which I had fixed for all these hours to be my goal.

It is the great platform just over Barl'ton, whence all the world lies out before one. Eastward into the night for fifty miles stretched on the walls of the Downs, and it stretched westward towards the coloured sky where a full but transfigured daylight still remained. Southwards was the belt of the sea, very broad, as it is from these bare heights, and absolutely still; nor did any animal move in the brushwood near me to insult the majesty of that silence. Northward before me and far below swept the Weald.

It has been suggested that the four men are all aspects of Belloc himself; but I do not see any reason to believe this, except in so far as all creations are aspects of their creator. Grizzlebeard, The Sailor, and The Poet stand out distinct and clear, albeit their distinction is achieved primarily through visual description rather than through speech. We see Grizzlebeard, tall, lean bearded, " well on in years, vigorous; his eyes were deep set in his head; they were full of travel and of sadness"; and the Sailor—" a very jovial fellow," whose eyes were " veiled with the salt of the sea, and paler than the eyes of a landsman would have been"; and The Poet " with his eyes arched and large as though in a perpetual surprise;" his " long limbs seemed to have loose joints, his arms dangled rather than swang, he steered no very straight course along the road, and under his felt hat with its narrow brim there hung tawny hair much too long and in no way vigorous." But when they speak, the language—the phraseology, the choice of words—is almost identical: it is Myself speaking. We cannot say whether Belloc intended this or not; but whatever his intention he has succeeded in keeping the characters separate by the visual method, while suggesting their spiritual affinity in their speech. Although Belloc is not a master of fiction, as a humanist he takes a delight in the portrayal of character. As an historian and sociologist he analyses character within the framework of thought; but as an essayist and novelist he describes character in terms of what he imaginatively *sees*, and the success of *The Four Men* is largely due to visual characterization. The travellers live, and once we have journeyed with them from Rother to Arun they are our companions for life.

Whether or no the four men are aspects of Belloc, it is significant that he has selected four eternal types of Englishmen—a country gentleman, a sailor, a poet, and most significantly, himself. All are free men of strong individuality embodying the spirit of Catholic humanism that has never quite died out of this land. And if ever the darkness of the totalitarian night were to overwhelm us, that spirit would remain. Somewhere, I believe, we should find Grizzlebeard sitting in the quiet of a country house and talking of lost love and departed beauty, and hear The Sailor roaring out his songs in some forgotten inn within sound of the sea, and The Poet muttering his divine nonsense in the woodlands of the South. Somewhere we should find Myself, arguing endlessly, and drinking pre-totalitarian port.

The journey of the four men at All Hallows takes its significance from the duality of human nature with its roots in the change and decay of earth and its breath from the everlasting world of the spirit. Christianity, and Catholic Christianity above all, has enabled us to transcend this duality in the personality of Christ and in the sacramental system; but so long as we sojourn upon earth, nothing can altogether remove the conflict at the heart of our being, and we should be less than human if we did not look back regretfully at the fields and woods of home before the clouds of immortality encompass us for ever. For we are earth-bound and heaven-gazing: atheists at heart, theists in head; and only certain great saints such as Francis of Assisi have perfectly united the love of earth and the love of God.

The essential Catholic humanism that integrates the earthly and the spiritual informs *The Four Men,* and gives it its deep significance and beauty. From one angle it might almost embody the mood of Hardy and Housman—the mood of earth-sadness, and of grief for that which must perish utterly and return no more. Behind the laughter and songs of the four men is the prescience of loss, a prescience deepened by the allusions throughout the book to departed youth and the passing of friends. Elsewhere Belloc has written that the things that endure most in this bad world are " laughter and the love of friends "; but here, though the laughter is loud and long, and the love of the four friends of the road as deep as if they had known each other all their lives, we know that at the end there must be bereavement, emptiness, and silence. This strange atheistic and pessimistic earth-sadness, with its haunting cadences of regret, its intimately-entwined fruition and loss—a fruition that seems deeper and lovelier because of the loss to come—is a peculiarly English thing. We find it not only in the poets, but in such essentially English musicians as Vaughan Williams and Butterworth. It is a note that sounds through much of Belloc's work.

Genuine unbelief leads to frustration; hence perhaps why those who have not believed have rarely attained to universal greatness. Their work is as limited as their narrow material universe. But the greatness of *The Four Men* is that it expresses all that the pessimists feel so deeply, while yet being illumined with the hope that springs from faith. Without faith there can be no hope, and without the creative vitality generated by hope there can be no true charity nor lasting love. The ultimate Faith that shines through the pages of *The Four Men* does not destroy the earthly sense of transience, but redeems it. Religion alone can save the experience that the unbelieving pagan values. Totalitarianism is the enemy of the pagan, no less than the Christian, humanist; and only where the Faith remains will there be a world in which the pagan can enjoy his tears.

All these essays and miscellaneous writings of Belloc reveal the quality of his prose to a high degree. Its rhythm, simplicity and strength, its *vigour*—perhaps that is the word that best describes it—and its consistency through all the many forms in which it is expressed, are unique in modern English literature. " In his best work," says the *Concise Cambridge History of English Literature*, " Belloc is the best prose writer of the period." His prose has something of the quality of the *Iliad*. It is in complete harmony with contemporary expression; but it is also timeless.

THE POET

IF the historian and sociologist represent the thinker, and the essayist the man of letters, the poet reveals the artist in Belloc. But while greatly admiring much of his verse I do not find myself fully qualified to judge it. Poetry is a specialized art, and the final judgment of Belloc's verse must rest with the specialist. I can only give an opinion as an ordinary lover of good verse (though of somewhat limited range and taste), and I must confess that I find it difficult to go all the way with those who regard Belloc as a great poet. I am quite unable to understand the few who regard him as primarily a poet. There can be no doubt that he possesses great poetical sensibility; but I contend that the poet in him is best expressed in his inspired lines of prose. For such an

artist prose is not always enough, and from time to time it
overflows into poetry: hence there is always a prose quality
about even his finest poems. He has produced a quantity
of inspired verse, among which are one or two gems that
would make the reputation of many a minor poet. Yet I
doubt if this entitles him to be called a major poet; for
two reasons. The first concerns his attitude to poetry: the
second concerns the nature of poetry itself.

First, then, it seems to me that no man for whom poetry
is incidental is, in the truest sense, a poet. It is said that
Belloc is devoted to poetry, and that he rates his own verse
high among his achievements. Elsewhere, however, he has
affirmed that history is his greatest interest and most
significant work—a view that seems to me, for reasons given
earlier on, nearer to the truth. A poet is one who, like
Tennyson, Wordsworth, and Eliot, devotes himself primarily
to poetry as his life's work. It is difficult to recall any great
poet for whom poetry has been incidental.

Second, the nature of poetry. Great poetry springs from
what for want of a better word, we must call mysticism;
from what Maritain calls a " natural mystical experience"
that expresses itself in signs and symbols. In this connexion,
even so-called philosophical poetry is always symbolic.
Now mysticism is a quality in which Belloc seems to me
to be lacking. Mysticism, as I have said, has no part in
his religion. His deepest inspiration derives from human
stimulus—that is, *man* in relation to the Faith and the land
and this quality of mind essentially flowers in fine prose.
Poetry—as Belloc recognizes in his portrait of The Poet in
The Four Men—is the expression of the seer and visionary.
The poet, as poet, is always, in the best sense, a little mad.
Although this view derives from the prosaic Aristotle
whose teaching on art has given rise to the belief that
poetry and madness are allied, there is some truth in it.
Belloc, even when most inspired, is always very sane.

Belloc's verse falls roughly into three divisions: sonnets,
miscellaneous verse and epigrams, and humorous verse.
The sonnets are fine; but I doubt if they would have made
his reputation. Some of his most perfect verse is to be
found among the miscellaneous pieces such as *The Birds*,

and *The Early Morning*. Here we have two aspects of
Belloc that continually recur throughout his work: the
religious and the pastoral. But always the human element
is predominant. The religious poems are centred in the
person of Christ, and Our Lady and the saints; the nature
poems have either, like *A Shropshire Lad*, a human background, or are expressed in human similes and associations.

> The moon on the one hand, the dawn on the other:
> The moon is my sister, the dawn is my brother.
> The moon on my left, and the dawn on my right,
> My brother, good morning: my sister, good night.

The beauty and simplicity of such lines is uncapturable:
they distil the essential coolness and stillness of early
morning. They are pure Belloc, as also is this epigram
which represents him at his very best.

> When we are dead, some Hunting-boy will pass
> And find a stone half-hidden in tall grass
> And grey with age: but having seen that stone
> (Which was your image), ride more slowly on.

The spirit of the English countryside shines through many
of his most inspired lines.

> The trees that grow in my own country
>   Are the beech tree and the yew;
> Many stand together,
>   And some stand few.
> In the month of May in my own country
>   All the woods are new.

Belloc's command of words is remarkable, and in some of
his humorous verse reaches a very high level. All his wit
and irony and devastating knowledge of human nature are
here, in verses of which the *Lines to a Don* is one of the
most brilliant examples. I quote the first part:

> Remote and ineffectual Don
> That dared attack my Chesterton,
> With that poor weapon, half-impelled,
> Unlearnt, unsteady, hardly held,
> Unworthy for a tilt with men—
> Your quavering and corroded pen;
> Don poor at Bed and worse at Table,
> Don pinched, Don starved, Don miserable;
> Don stuttering, Don with roving eyes,
> Don nervous, Don of crudities;
> Don clerical, Don ordinary,
> Don self-absorbed and solitary;

Don here-and-there, Don epileptic;
Don puffed and empty, Don dyspeptic;
Don middle-class, Don sycophantic,
Don dull, Don brutish, Don pedantic;
Don hypocritical, Don bad,
Don furtive, Don three-quarters mad;
Don (since a man must make an end),
Don that shall never be my friend.

In his humorous verse Belloc's genius for hitting exactly the right phrase to express some human absurdity is displayed in the highest degree. It reveals his remarkable synthesis of Gallic and English elements which combines a cultivated wit and irony with an inspired horseplay and a delight in sheer nonsense.

In Belloc the poet we see yet another aspect of Belloc the Catholic humanist. His verse is not only an expression of his profoundly humanistic spirit but is related to the rest of his work by the things it affirms and the things it satirizes. It affirms a joyous faith in God and man, and a profound love of the earth, above all the English earth; and it satirizes the enemies of those things, bureaucracy, secularism, big business, and the rest. Belloc's verse is incidental; but it is an incident of deep significance in his work as a whole.

CONCLUSIONS

Throughout the course of this brief Introduction I have tried to indicate the inner unity of Belloc's spirit, and the emergence of that spirit in the variegated pattern of his work. I have rejected the view that regards his work as unco-ordinated and over-versatile, and have argued that it reveals the inner unity of an innate humanism, receiving its fulfillment in the objective social life of the Church, and expressing itself formally in history and sociology and over-flowing into essays and verse. It may be that only a man who is so much of a piece could afford to be so wide in range: a less integral character would be lost outside his own limited sphere. Belloc has extended his range too widely, and he has written too much; but there is no living writer

comparable to him in the relatively high quality of so wide
a range and so vast a quantity of work. If I have done
nothing more than indicate the essential underlying unity of
his work I shall be content. No one can please all admirers
of Belloc: those who admire one aspect of him frequently
conflict with those who admire another; but I hope that my
own view is broad enough to ensure a just evaluation of the
quality of the whole. In conclusion, I should like to say
something about his position and influence in the contemporary English-speaking world.

Belloc has always enjoyed a very high reputation as a
man of letters in this country, but until very recently his
reputation and influence as a thinker has been underrated.
The reason is obvious. Although he has spoken to us in
accents of the highest literary art, his has been a lone voice
in the modern wilderness of unbelief, abstraction and
mechanization. But of recent years a slow and almost
imperceptible change has begun to take place in the views
of many of our prominent writers and ideologists. As
we saw in considering *The Servile State*, the emergence of
materialism from theory into practice has impressed its real
nature upon us. Men of good-will who were prepared to
argue for a secular society have been forced, by the horrors
of materialism in act to reconsider their position. The
result is that to-day the fundamental things that Belloc
stands for—religion, humanism, distributism—are being
reasserted by many who hitherto dismissed him as a crank.
The turn of the tide is so subtle a movement as to be almost
imperceptible, and we are now at that moment in history
when, although the totalitarian recession seems to be
inexorable, there are signs that the tide is turning and the
spirit of man moving once more towards the shores of faith.

Among those contemporary Englishmen whose change of
outlook gives us hope in the rising tide, are such men as
T. S. Eliot, Middleton Murry, Aldous Huxley, Gerald
Heard, and C. E. M. Joad—all writers of intensely different
personalities and modes of expression. One of the first to
see the new vision was T. S. Eliot, whose *Waste Land* was
a protest against the soulless desert of scepticism and despair
that has so largely paved the way for totalitarianism.

Eliot has found integration in Anglo-Catholicism, and his later works have an affirmative note. Middleton Murry has moved from atheistic communism to an undenominational Christianity that is yet deeply devotional, and for communism has substituted a way of life based upon the family, the community, the land, and creative work. Chesterton, in one of his vivid flashes of prophetic intuition, wrote of Murry, that on finding God a very difficult problem, he " illogically said *Adieu,* but God said *au revoir.*" Aldous Huxley has moved from the lower psychology of moods to the higher psychology of mysticism. Although he is still far from the Catholic humanism of Belloc, his deep theocentrism is a portent for our time, as is also his belief in the small community as the political and sociological norm. Gerald Heard has followed a very similar path, but from the starting point of materialistic science rather than psychology. C. E. M. Joad, from the standpoint of philosophy, has moved towards a deeper understanding of the Christian view, and his socialistic outlook has undergone some significant changes in the direction of distributism. It is significant that D. H. Lawrence, the prophet of irrationality, the apostle of the dark night of the body, saw dimly the light of Christianity and community before his death.

All these contemporaries of Belloc have moved towards his religious and distributist position; but lacking the humanist centre of the Faith they have, with the exception of Eliot, tended to an unorthodox position in religion. The Faith, as Belloc himself has pointed out, is a mean, and heresy is always a form of extremism. Murry over-personalizes religion and thus loses sight of the objective structure which alone can preserve personality. Huxley and Heard have adopted a position of extreme all-or-nothing mysticism. Joad, of a more worldly mentality than the others, has tried to keep one foot in the secular camp of his youth while tentatively putting the tip of the other into the stream of eternal life. Nevertheless the significant fact remains, that all these men have come to something very like Belloc's religious-distributist position; and I think that the chief cause has been the totalitarian attack upon man.

But the only effective answer to totalitarianism is Catholic humanism.

The older men, such as W. H. Hudson, Galsworthy and Bernard Shaw, followed their own ways. Hudson's great vision of nature lacked the vitalizing force of religious faith; though in his social outlook he was akin to Belloc. Galsworthy was too hidebound in late Victorian liberalism to have much in common with a Catholic humanist, while Shaw, with his creative evolution and desire to tidy up the world is perhaps farther removed from the humanist spirit than any of the others.

The man who came most under the direct influence of Belloc was his great friend Chesterton. Though similar in outlook and tastes the resemblances between them were superficial. Belloc's influence upon Chesterton's thought was enormous; but Chesterton was an original genius who gave an entirely new and distinctive character to their common fund of ideas. The Chesterbelloc is a myth. In character, temperament, and literary style the two men were the opposite of each other. Chesterton, though a humanist, was much more of a metaphysician and a mystic. Where Belloc is logical, Chesterton is speculative; where Belloc is factual, Chesterton is fanciful; where Belloc is objective, Chesterton is imaginative. In style Chesterton is flamboyant where Belloc is economical; and even when Belloc is flamboyant, as in his lighter works, he is always sparing in language. Chesterton's prose at its worst is highly-coloured journalese: Belloc, even in his work as a journalist, never writes journalese. Chesterton will end an essay on the open spaces with the sentence, " And as the stars came out above the plain I wept for Walham Green "—and he probably did, for he was at heart a Cockney, and never had Belloc's enduring love of the English earth.

Apart from Chesterton, a group of Catholic writers, prominent among whom are Christopher Dawson, Christopher Hollis and E. I. Watkin, have developed many of the ideas latent in Belloc's message, Dawson in the field of history, Hollis in the field of sociology, and Watkin in the field of philosophy. The only writer known to me who has been stylistically as well as intellectually influenced by

Belloc is J. B. Morton, many passages from whose writings have an unmistakably Bellocian flavour.

To-day, when the menace of totalitarianism is greater than ever before, Belloc's reputation and influence as a thinker is growing. But what of the future? How will he stand in English literature a generation hence? Everything depends upon the religious and social condition of society. If the tide flows and men return to sanity, Belloc will stand out as one of the great minds of the age and a prose writer of genius. But if the tide ebbs still farther from the shore of the Faith, leaving only the dried bones of what were once living men, he will inevitably suffer an eclipse. Even the splendour of his prose will suffer, for it is inspired by the things for which he stands—the Faith, mankind, community, the land—and if these go, good prose will go with them. Already the arid jargon of left-wing philosophy, literature, and art is a portent.

But the things for which he stands will never be altogether eclipsed, for they are endemic to human nature. The more fully and integrally human in the Christian sense men are, the more significant will life become. There is a danger that in reaction against the inhuman materialism of our time, men may turn to an all-or-nothing mysticism such as that advocated by Huxley and Heard. It is a very real danger; because in spite of the enormous power and value of mysticism, it can, if regarded as the only way, lead to apathy, and thereby play into the hands of totalitarianism. The integral humanism of the Catholic Church is the only effective challenge to the inhumanism of our time. It is founded upon the stupendous fact that God Himself is a humanist, since He paid man the supreme compliment of the Incarnation. From the Incarnation radiates the sanctification of the entire cosmos and of all human life and activity. It is not the simple and often absurd things (which Aldous Huxley calls, rather contemptuously, life's " imbecilities ") which are wrong, but the use we make of them. Every trivial act can be sanctified in the crucible of true humanism—that Christ-centred humanism of which Belloc is one of the supreme advocates, and which explains why he can write with such joy about the smallest things. The

D

modern world is losing this joy in life. It is fast being reduced to the freezing point of ultimate abstraction. Behaviourism has emasculated the individual, physics has dissolved nature, metaphysics has annihilated God, and economics has reduced the living community to a machine.

The secret of Belloc's greatness is the depth and richness of his humanity which proceeds from the love of One who was both God and man. Somewhere in *Hills and the Sea* occurs this most revealing sentence: " It may be taken that whatever form truth takes among men will be the more perfect in proportion as the men who receive that form are more fully men." There speaks the humanist; and there also by implication, speaks the Catholic humanist. For the men who " are more fully men " are those who have received the Faith in which human nature attains to its full stature.

SUPPLEMENT I: SYNOPSIS

The spirit of Belloc is Catholic humanism informing the varied body of his work — confusion concerning the word humanism — broadly, humanism a psychological and individual view of life—humanism stresses the logical, empirical, emotional, rather than the mystical or mechanical—humanism of Belloc—his logic, empiricism, and sense of history—his attitude to the Faith—to science—his scepticism—the ontological argument—the humanist mentality inborn, but flourishes in a favourable soil—the transcendentalism of the Orient and the totalitarianism of the modern West are both inhuman—only two genuinely humanist societies in history: the Graeco-Roman and the Christian—Belloc's feeling for the classics—wide distinction between pagan and Christian humanism—the natural man and the supernatural man—Christian humanism centred in the person of Christ: *humanisme intégral* — importance of Christian teaching on dual nature of man—emasculation of the humanist spirit in the modern world—pagan and Christian humanism alike in holding a balanced joy in life—the true Christian neither conventional nor an enthusiast—Belloc's joy in all life characteristic of his Catholic humanism—humanism of the Faith brought out by the choice of Peter as head of the Church, the typical human being with all his virtues and faults—the gay and gallant company of Christian saints—humanism of the Middle Ages—the symbolic Gothic cathedral—Belloc's mediaevalism—answer to those who criticise him as being archaic—he stands for the truths that the Middle Ages enshrined—modern totalitarianism the result of secularism derived from the Renaissance and idealism derived from the Reformation—their reciprocal effect—secular humanism inadequate—leads to egoism and despair—humanism of the Catholic countries, especially France—Belloc's French and English ancestry—effect of his heredity on his thought and style—but he remains fundamentally English.

By bent and training Belloc primarily an historian—his credentials for writing history—humanism and history closely related—limitations of metaphysical and scientific history—the psychological essence of history—Belloc's psychological approach—psychological history is exposed to the charge of bias and inaccuracy, but has a truth of its own—inadequacy of a merely behaviouristic psychology—it requires an artist such as Belloc to get to the roots of human personality—for Belloc, the interplay of personalities is decisive in history—difficulties arising from psychological history—if it is hard to judge one whom we know now, how can we judge many in the past?—Belloc's answer is that the past gives us psychological perspective—accusation of bias against Belloc—those who bring it often themselves biased —the unfamiliarity of his position and the force with which he expresses himself partly responsible for the charge—his humanism a source of strength and weakness as an historian —realism of his psychological judgments—the idealist and scientist do not view man realistically: only the Christian humanist can see man as he is—in Belloc's history, the past is re-experienced in the readers' mind—he also excels in the description of battles—his military experience and know-ledge—his English and French historical works—the *History of England*, and the *Shorter History*—the studies of *Charles I* and *Cromwell*—Belloc's imperfect judgment of Cromwell—his great studies of the leaders of the French Revolution—tendency to over-simplification in dealing with impersonal issues—exaggeration of the effect of the money power—*Europe and the Faith*—Belloc a genuine historian, and history his greatest achievement.

History and sociology closely related—Belloc's sociology the most perfect expression of his humanism—he stands for the individual, property, the land—his sociology is called *distributism*—nature of distributism—unlike capitalism, socialism, and anarchism which have to be imposed upon society, distributism is the ground of society, and grows out of the psychological needs of mankind—Belloc's sociological treatise, *The Servile State*, is closely bound up with his view of history—it discovers the origins of capitalism in the Reformation—socialism is not the remedy but the cul-

mination of capitalism—both end in the Servile State—
materialist totalitarianism has proved Belloc's forecast
right—theoretical and practical materialism—the logic of
totalitarianism is unanswerable on materialist premises—
though it must fail in the end, totalitarianism may become
established for centuries—*The Servile State* is chiefly
effective as a broad survey—Belloc not a detailed thinker—
his unsatisfactory treatment of the problem of freedom and
happiness—the *Essay on the Restoration of Property* a
supplement to *Servile State*—*Servile State* theoretical, the
Essay a plan of action—*Essay*, on the whole, pessimistic—
Belloc never allows his sense of the realities of human
nature to be over-ridden by his ideals—insight, realism, and
honesty of his sociological works—his ideal, a Christian
distributist society.

Belloc's Essays and Miscellaneous Writings include many
forms: literature, satire, travel, controversy—all are closely
related to his historical and sociological position—the collec-
tions of essays proper—their humanistic spirit—the *On* series
—Belloc's humour in the short essay—his irony and sense of
fun—humour often close to sorrow—relation of humour
and humanism—lack of humour in idealism and materialism— biological and psychological nature of humour—
humourlessness of art and science—humour and the Fall
of Man— Belloc has poked fun at most things but he has
reverence—his attitude to the Faith, and incident of
hearing Mass in *The Path to Rome*—*The Four Men* a
microcosm of his whole outlook—the setting and story of
The Four Men— its deeply humanistic significance—it en-
shrines the problem of our spiritual kinship with God and
our physical roots in the earth—greatness of Belloc's prose.

Belloc as poet—he has written much fine verse, but not a
great poet in the complete sense of the word—predominantly
a prose writer whose prose overflows into inspired verse—
his verse always has a prose quality—no great poet produces
poetry incidentally—Belloc's verse lacks the visionary
quality that goes with poetic genius—form of his verse: the
sonnets, the miscellaneous verse, the epigrams and humorous verse—great beauty of his religious and pastoral poems
—the humorous verse: its brilliance and power—his genius

for finding exactly the right words to express human absurdity—his verse a significant expression of his Catholic humanism.

Summing up—inner unity of Belloc's spirit and external unity of his work—his reputation among his contemporaries high as a writer but, until recently, he has been underrated as a thinker—his lone voice in the modern world—but the menace of totalitarianism has forced many of his contemporaries to come round to the things he stands for— they are mostly younger men—the men of his own generation are less influenced—Belloc's influence on Chesterton, but the two men very different in temperament and style—the work of certain Catholic writers in sympathy with Belloc—the future of Belloc, depends upon the future of the world—but whatever the future, the things for which he stands are permanent.

SUPPLEMENT II: A LIST OF BELLOC'S WORKS

The following list of Belloc's works is, as far as I am
aware, complete. Apart from his own books, Belloc has
made some important translations, and has edited, and
contributed to, a number of publications; but I have not
thought it necessary to mention these. A glance at the list
below reveals the immensity of Belloc's output. There are
well over a hundred books, the majority of them sub-
stantial works of several hundred pages each. Some have
had more than one publisher, and many have gone into
several editions; but a number are out of print for the time
being. In my list I have confined myself to stating the title
of the book and the publisher or publishers. The arrangement of the books is not chronological, but follows the
broad scheme outlined in the foregoing pages, i.e., History,
Sociology, Essays and Miscellaneous Writings, Verse. The
advantages of this, as I have said, is that it reveals the inner
harmony of Belloc's work. Apart from this, however, the
nature of the work is against a chronological treatment,
since there is no marked development of intellectual and
literary power in Belloc from youth to old age. From the
start, he seems to have found himself, and to have gone on
continually at much the same level of output and inspiration.
No purpose, then, would be served by a chronological divi-
sion with dates; but considerable order is achieved by the
logical method I have followed here. Thus wherever
necessary I have subdivided the work in each main group;
and the order of books within each subdivision follows a
broad scheme based upon what I conceive to be, as nearly
as possible, their logical relation. It will be observed that
many of Belloc's books on the Catholic Faith come under
History, since his main approach to the Faith is, as we have
seen, humanistic and historical, while others come under
Controversy.

HISTORY

Belloc's historical works may be conveniently divided into English History (his largest consistent output, and greatest achievement), French History, and History in General. Under the first two, English and French History, I have given first the comprehensive works, and afterwards—in historical order—the biographical studies of kings, statesmen, and the rest. Under History in General, I have arranged the books in the following order: World History, Europe, The Catholic Church, Modern History (The first World War, etc.).

ENGLISH HISTORY

A History of England (4 Vols., to 1612)	Methuen
A Shorter History of England (1 Vol.)	Harrap
William the Conqueror	{ Peter Davies / Nelson
The Book of the Bayeaux Tapestry ..	Chatto & Windus
Wolsey	Cassell
Cranmer	Cassell
Elizabethan Commentary	Cassell
Charles I	Cassell
Cromwell	Cassell
Oliver Cromwell	Benn
The Last Rally (Charles II) ..	Cassell
James II	Faber & Faber
The Tactics and Strategy of the Great Duke of Marlborough ..	Arrowsmith
Warfare in England	Williams & Norgate
Six British Battles	Arrowsmith

FRENCH HISTORY

Miniatures of French History	Nelson
Joan of Arc	Cassell
Richelieu	Benn
Monarchy: A Study of Louis XIV	Cassell
The Last Days of the French Monarchy	Chapman & Hall
The French Revolution	Williams & Norgate
Marie Antoinette	Methuen
Robespierre: A Study	Nisbet
Danton: A Study	{ Nisbet Nelson
Napoleon	Cassell
The Campaign of 1812 and the Retreat from Moscow	Nelson

HISTORY IN GENERAL

The Crisis of our Civilization	Cassell
Europe and the Faith	Constable
The Catholic Church and History	Burns Oates
The Great Heresies	Sheed & Ward
The Crusade: The World's Debate	Cassell
How the Reformation Happened	Cape
Characters of the Reformation	Sheed & Ward
The Battle Ground (Syria and Holy Land)	Cassell
A General Sketch of the European War (2 Vols.)	Burrup, Mathieson & Sprague
The Two Maps of Europe (Great War)	Pearson
The Stane Street	Constable

SOCIOLOGY

A considerable number of Belloc's sociological writings are scattered in the pages of various journals to which he has contributed from time to time during the last 40 years, such as The Eye Witness, G.K.'s Weekly, The Weekly Review, Truth, etc. His sociological books represent a comparatively small part of his output. I have arranged them to show the development of his fundamental position (as set out in *The Servile State*) in many varied fields.

The Servile State	Foulis Constable
Socialism and the Servile State ..	Independent Labour Party
An Essay on the Restoration of Property	Distributist League
The Party System (with Cecil Chesterton)	Swift
The House of Commons and Monarchy	Allen & Unwin
The Liberal Tradition	Cassell
An Essay on the Nature of Contemporary England	Constable
The Eye-Witness	Eveleigh Nash
The Free Press	Allen & Unwin
The Catholic and the War	Burns Oates
The Jews	Constable
The Contrast (Europeans and Americans)	Arrowsmith
Economics for Helen	Arrowsmith

ESSAYS AND MISCELLANEOUS WORKS

The Essays and Miscellaneous writings comprise the largest number of Belloc's books. With the exception of the controversial books, they represent on the whole the lighter side of his work. Among them, however, are some examples of his greatest writing in the literary and artistic as opposed to the ideological sphere. Apart from the Essays proper I have divided the Miscellaneous Works into Travel and Topography, Literary Criticism, Fiction, Satire and Humour, Controversy. Anyone familiar with Belloc's outlook will see how closely related are Satire and Humour to his works of Controversy: hence the position in which I have placed them. Most of the controversial works are concerned with the Catholic Faith; and though it would be possible to regard some of them as belonging more to History or Sociology, I have put them in this position since they are primarily controversial in character.

ESSAYS

On Nothing and Kindred Subjects ..	Methuen
On Something	Methuen
On Anything	{ Constable Methuen
On Everything	Methuen
On	Methuen
This and That and the Other ..	Methuen
First and Last	Methuen
Hills and the Sea	Methuen
The Silence of the Sea	Cassell
Places	Cassell
A Conversation with an Angel ..	Cape
A Conversation with a Cat.. ..	Cassell
Short Talks with the Dead and Others	{ Cayme Press Sheed & Ward
The Aftermath	Duckworth

TRAVEL AND TOPOGRAPHY

The Four Men (A Farrago)	Nelson
The County of Sussex	Cassell
The Path to Rome	{ Allen & Unwin { Nelson
Paris	{ Arnold { Methuen
The Pyrenees	Methuen
Esto Perpetua (North Africa) ..	Duckworth
Many Cities	Constable
The Old Road	Constable
The Road	T. Fisher Unwin
The Highway and its Vehicles ..	The Studio
The River of London	Foulis
The Historic Thames	Dent
On Sailing the Sea	Methuen
The Cruise of the Nona	Constable
Return to the Baltic	Constable

LITERARY CRITICISM

On Translation	Clarendon Press
Milton	Cassell
On the Place of Gilbert Chesterton in English Letters	Sheed & Ward
Avril (The Poetry of the French Renaissance)	Duckworth Sheed & Ward

FICTION

Belinda	Constable
Mr. Clutterbuck's Election ..	{ Eveleigh Nash { Nelson
Pongo and the Bull	Constable
A Change in the Cabinet	Methuen
But Soft ! We are Observed ..	{ Harmondsworth { Arrowsmith { Penguin Books
Emanuel Burden, Merchant ..	Methuen
The Girondin	Nelson
The Missing Masterpiece	Arrowsmith
Mr. Petre	Arrowsmith
The Mercy of Allah	Chatto & Windus
The Hedge and the Horse	Cassell
The Green Overcoat	Arrowsmith
The Haunted House	Arrowsmith
The Man who made Gold ..	Arrowsmith
The Postermaster General ..	Arrowsmith
The Emerald of Catherine the Great	Arrowsmith

SATIRE AND HUMOUR

Mrs. Markham's New History of England	Cayme Press
The Great Inquiry	Duckworth
Nine Nines	Blackwell

CONTROVERSY

Most of Belloc's controversial works deal with some aspect of the Catholic Faith. His positive and constructive contributions to Catholic thought are found mainly in the pages of his historical writings. The works below are, for the most part, critical, defensive, and polemical—with the possible exception of *The Question and the Answer*.

Essays of a Catholic Layman in England	Sheed & Ward
The Question and the Answer ..	Longmans
Survivals and New Arrivals ..	Sheed & Ward
An Open Letter on the Decay of Faith	Burns Oates
A Companion to Wells' " Outline of History "	Sheed & Ward
Mr. Belloc Still Objects to Mr. Wells' " Outline of History "	Sheed & Ward
The Case of Dr. Coulton	Sheed & Ward

VERSE

The bulk of Belloc's verse, Sonnets, Miscellaneous Pieces, and Humorous Verse, has been collected in two volumes which I have placed at the head of the list. The original separate books follow. The rest of his verse is to be found in some of the Essays and Miscellaneous Works.

Sonnets and Verse (Collected Sonnets and Miscellaneous Pieces) ..	Duckworth
Cautionary Verses (Collected Humorous Verse)	Duckworth
Verses	Duckworth
Verses and Sonnets	Ward & Downey
An Heroic Poem in Praise of Wine ..	Peter Davies
The Modern Traveller	Arnold
A Chanty of the Nona	Faber & Gwyer
New Cautionary Tales	Duckworth
The Bad Child's Book of Beasts ..	Duckworth
More Beasts for Worse Children ..	{ Arnold { Duckworth
More Peers	{ Swift { Duckworth
Ladies and Gentlemen	Duckworth
A Moral Alphabet	E. Arnold

47561

MADE AND PRINTED IN ENGLAND